THE MIDDLE PART OF
FAITH

THE MIDDLE PART OF
FAITH

PASTOR REGINALD MCNEESE

Walton Publishing House
Houston, Texas
www.waltonpublishinghouse.com

Printed in the United States of America

The advice found within may not be suitable for every individual. This work is purchased with the understanding that neither the author nor the publisher is held responsible for any results. Neither author nor publisher assumes responsibility for errors, omissions, or contrary interpretations of the subject matter herein. Any perceived disparagement of an individual or organization is a misinterpretation.

Brand and product names mentioned are trademarks that belong solely to their respective owners. Library of Congress Cataloging-in-Publication Data under

ISBN: 978-1-953993-41-0 (Paperback)
ISBN: 978-1-953993-40-3 (Digital/ E-book)

DEDICATION

This book is dedicated to those that do not follow the herd but follow their own path despite how popular and talented the herd is.

This book is dedicated to the underdogs and the unsung heroes, who are slow to speak and slow to react but hold their tongue and their peace until they have something valuable to contribute.

This book is dedicated to the lone wolf that is comfortable in their own skin and does not need the limelight or a crowd but can command them all if they need to.

This book is dedicated to those that focus on their business and are never concerned about the competition because they know they are in competition with only themselves.

This book is dedicated to those that do not try to keep up with the Joneses or engage in any trivial pursuits because they know who they are and have nothing to prove to anyone.

This book is dedicated to those that are strong-willed, steadfast focused people whose pursuits are paramount to another.

CONTENTS

PRAYER

ATHER IN HEAVEN, in the name of Jesus we thank you right now because we understand that we are studying your Word. It is our desire to enter into your glory and into your presence and learn the way to receive from You. Lord, as I minister your Word to those reading this book, I pray that it will penetrate all hearts and lodge in all minds of the reader. I pray they will be able to execute this Word and stand in your presence unhindered and unblocked by the enemy. I declare that the enemy will not be able to stop us any longer. In Jesus' name, Amen.

INTRODUCTION

What are you seeking from God?

> " So Jesus answered and said unto them, Have faith in God."
>
> Mark 11:22 NASV

AT THE BEGINNING of your faith journey, and operating within the plan and purpose of God, I am convinced that in order to receive from God you have to do things in a prescribed way, and in a prescribed manner. If you want to get anything from God, it must line up with the Word of God. God is a God of principle and order. This means you are not going to just do anything or say a quick prayer haphazardly and receive your petition. God does not operate that way. Receiving from Him takes planning and must also have a purpose.

Contrary to many beliefs, receiving from God is never activated by manipulation. In fact, receiving from God can only happen when we follow the instructions of our Heavenly Father as it is written in the Word. Whenever you come to God for a need to be met, you must come in faith. As we go further along in this book, I will show you examples of how faith works, how faith comes, and how to release your faith.

The Bible says in Hebrews 10:38 (KJV), "Now the just shall live by faith: but if any man draws back, my soul shall have no pleasure in him."

Therefore, if you are going to live by faith, you first need to know three (3) points.

#1 What faith is.
#2 How faith works.
#3 How to receive faith.

…The just shall live by faith.

As we dive into this book, we will discuss these three (3) areas and the practical application and principles of how faith works. It is important that you know the operations of faith. One of the main things you must know is that as we serve God, He only responds to faith. We must operate by the Kingdom of Heaven's principles of faith while we are living in this present world.

66 They are not of the world, even as I am not of this world."

John 17:16 (KJB)

In this book, I am going to share what happens during the most critical time in your faith walk with God- what often occurs in the faith journey. I believe during the middle part of faith, we simply need to continue to act in a prescribed way and manner from the beginning of our faith journey to the end of our faith journey. During the middle part of your faith journey is when you need the encouragement and empowerment to stand on God's Word and not waver or be in doubt. I am not saying it is easy, but it's a part of the journey of the life of the believer.

> 66 For therein is the righteousness of God revealed from faith to faith: as it is written, The just shall live by faith."
>
> Romans 1:17 (KJB)

Are you tired of going into cycles of setback and failure? Are you tired of letting the enemy defeat you? I want to admonish you to push past where you are today and pursue God like never before. Your faith will be built once you learn how faith works and how to apply it. For the past 17 years, I have been teaching on the principles of faith. As a pastor, I find so many believers have given up on faith and are living a life less than what God intended. I want your life to be different. I want you to get past the middle part of your faith journey because You have the Greater One living on the inside of you and you can live a victorious life.

Mark 11:22- 24 (KJV)

[22] "And Jesus answering saith unto them, Have faith in God."

[23] "For verily I say unto you, that whosoever shall say unto this mountain, be thou removed, and be thou cast into the sea; and shall not doubt in his heart, but shall believe that those things which he saith shall come to pass; he shall have whatsoever he saith."

[24] "Therefore I say unto you, what things soever ye desire when ye pray, believe that ye receive them, and ye shall have them."

CHAPTER ONE

Have Faith in God

HAVE YOU EVER read the story about Charles Atlas? Atlas was "the 90-pound weakling" who trained himself to develop his body from that of a weak man to becoming the most popular bodybuilder of his day. He only weighed about 97 pounds but will always be known as the powerhouse that changed the bodybuilding world. Because of his inability to gain weight, he discovered many of the muscle-building methods we now use today. Through his research, he studied the agility of lions and tigers and their power to jump over a school bus not vertically but horizontally. As he continued to study these animals with extreme power and agility, he set out on a life goal to become strong. He started going to the gym and he built his muscles and became an incredibly strong and smart man. Not only did he build his physical strength, but he also increased in wisdom and knowledge about how the human body works. Mr. Atlas went on to publish his applied wisdom in written publications that are now used by thousands of people who practice his exercise techniques to this day. He started off his "faith journey" in the arena of bodybuilding as a 90-pound weakling. What am I trying to tell you? I'm trying to tell you the faith that God has given you; the way to exercise that faith is to read and study the word and apply the word to your life. So, whenever problems come, and they will, you must constantly (exercise) your faith to get out of them.

What is Faith?

Faith is the ability to see and believe before you see the manifestation in the natural form. Faith is trusting and being fully persuaded to act on the Word of God. When the challenges in life arise, in which they do for everyone, your faith will keep you fully persuaded. When you operate in faith you are not halfway in and halfway out. Neither are you hanging on the fence in your thinking. Having faith means knowing that God is on your side and not only is He on your side, but He also wants you to win. As believers we can't settle, we must look past the idea that we are "just living in this world" or you are "just a sinner saved by grace." I remember when I first became a believer there was a popular Gospel song that people would sing in their churches. The lyrics were, "I'm just a 'nobody' trying to tell everybody about somebody." I despised those lyrics because I believe in God, we are somebodies. We are all created and formed in His image and likeness, which makes us somebody with a purpose and an assignment that must be fulfilled. Buying into this idea of being a "nobody" would mean that God made you be a nobody, and in faith, I know this to be different. This is the approach and firm belief I want you to take as you read this book. I want you to understand that you have been fully equipped and prepared to walk this life in victory.

You may say, "Well, you haven't really explained to me what faith is." Let me simplify this even more for you. Faith is firm confidence. Faith is being fully persuaded to whatever God has said. Without any doubt, you know and believe that He's able to perform. Having a firm or unyielding confidence or best explained as having a made-up mind in what God has promised you in the word. Your mind has to be so established that no other thoughts will steer you in another direction. That's what faith is. It's walking in your destiny and not allowing yourself to be separated from God.

While you are in the middle of your faith journey, waiting on your full manifestation, you must be fully persuaded that whatever He has said to you, about you, or for you, you can accomplish. The Word of God says you can and if the Word of God says that you can do all things through Christ who strengthens you, you can. Jesus would not tell you to do something that you weren't able to get accomplished. So, whatever you are facing right now, I want you to be encouraged. Whatever you are going through, whatever situation or circumstance is up against you, know that

God is on your side. He is on your side to help you walk in your purpose and fulfill the great work He has for you. As you build your faith, be fully persuaded that whatever God has promised, no matter what negative comes along with it, He's working it out for your good. Therefore, nothing can stop you and no weapon formed against you shall prosper. During any test in life our faith will be stretched, but it's up to us to push until we have received the victory.

The Measure of Faith

In the summer of 1989, a dear friend of mine was diagnosed with a terminal illness. He was someone I considered a great man of faith and although this illness took many of us by surprise, I knew he would overcome it. I had no doubt that he would pull through and receive his healing. He was a man that walked in kingdom dominion and authority in the healing anointing. He believed and spoke the word of God as he laid hands on the sick and he witnessed them healed. My friend was a firsthand witness to what the power of God, through faith in the Word could do. However, it was during the middle part of his faith journey that his faith began to decline. Despite his knowledge of the Word of God, when it was time to activate his faith for his own healing, he wasn't able to. Unfortunately, his health continued to decline, and the terminal illness overtook his body.

Before long, fear and doubt began to creep in, and he no longer had the faith to believe that God would heal him. My friend began listening to the negative words from his inner circle, and his family members planted seeds that were contrary to what Jesus spoke about faith and healing. He continued to stay in an environment that didn't operate in faith, and he listened to his family members who reminded him that his aunt and uncle died from the same health complications, and he would too. I found it quite interesting that he believed his family and friends as opposed to believing what the Word of God said. Despite the knowledge he had and the personal faith experiences he encountered, when it came down to him believing and receiving for himself, he had a "faith failure." Sadly, he died with the power of God residing on the inside of him and he never experienced the healing that he had seen manifested in others.

This is what happens to many believers who give up because the fight in the middle seems too hard. The middle part of your faith journey is a period when fear, doubt, and unbelief will show up and cause you to question God and/or His Word because of what the circumstances appear to be in your life. The middle part of faith is the time when most people have what I call a "faith failure." During a faith failure, people believe various false narratives such as the Word of God does not work, or they believe that they personally do not have strong enough faith to receive. They believe that somehow God is punishing them for something they have done wrong. They become discouraged and distracted by the cares of this world and often they never access the reward they rightfully deserve. In their mind God is teaching them humility, as if they are too high-minded to receive the things, they are asking God for.

I share these stories because I believe it doesn't matter if you know every scripture in the Bible, or if you don't apply faith to your life, you will be defeated. I felt compelled to write this book to keep the people of God on track. We teach faith from the pulpit on Sunday and the congregation receives a temporary uplift, but they are challenged with how to walk this out every day of their life. Faith is a journey. It's easy to have faith at the start and at the end of a situation. But it's the middle part that's most challenging.

In Matthew 14, Peter had his own personal encounter in the middle part of his faith journey. He was on the boat with the disciples when he saw Jesus' walking on the water.

Matthew 14: 22- 31 (KJV)

²² And straightway Jesus constrained his disciples to get into a ship, and to go before him unto the other side, while he sent the multitudes away.

²³ And when he had sent the multitudes away, he went up into a mountain apart to pray: and when the evening was come, he was there alone.

²⁴ But the ship was now in the midst of the sea, tossed with waves: for the wind was contrary.

²⁵ And in the fourth watch of the night Jesus went unto them, walking on the sea.

²⁶ And when the disciples saw him walking on the sea, they were troubled, saying, It is a spirit; and they cried out for fear.

²⁷ But straightway Jesus spake unto them, saying, Be of good cheer; it is I; be not afraid.

²⁸ And Peter answered him and said, Lord, if it be thou, bid me come unto thee on the water.

²⁹ And he said, Come. And when Peter was come down out of the ship, he walked on the water, to go to Jesus.

³⁰ But when he saw the wind boisterous, he was afraid; and beginning to sink, he cried, saying, Lord, save me.

³¹ And immediately Jesus stretched forth his hand, and caught him, and said unto him, O thou of little faith, wherefore didst thou doubt?

Jesus bade Peter to join him and for a split moment Peter did just that. His faith caused him to step out on that water. But stepping out of the boat was the beginning part of faith. Where Jesus was standing in the water a far off, represented the end where he would receive the promise of faith and reach the finish line. However, before he could get to the end, the middle part required him to walk on water. It was at that moment that doubt arose and he began to sink. Now we could look at this story of Peter and shake our head in disbelief. How could anyone who had their eyes on Jesus be concerned about drowning? It's apparent that he trusted Jesus, or he would have never stepped out of the boat in the first place.

But if we are honest, doesn't his story seem like many believers today? While they are in the middle part of faith, they become distracted by the worst-case scenario instead of the faith scenario. Enduring the middle part and coming out victorious on the other side is not for the faint of heart. On our faith journey, God will often ask us to do some things that are unfamiliar and uncomfortable to us. Oftentimes the thing that He requires of us will challenge you to push your way through to your promise. This can be an opportunity that is outside of your current skill set, knowledge level or area where you are comfortable. This can be physical or mental, it can be in a relationship. No matter what, God has called us to walk through our faith journey as overcomers. By faith you have everything you need, and you are more than able to accomplish anything.

I wrote this book to give you other resources to help take you from the beginning of your faith journey to the middle part and on to your manifested promise. God is calling you out into the middle. The place where He alone knows the coordinates. You don't get a map or compass in the middle part of faith. All we have is His Word and a track record of Him taking you through.

> 66 For I say, through the grace given unto me, to every man that is among you, not to think of himself more highly than he ought to think; but to think soberly, according as God hath dealt to every man the measure of faith."
>
> Romans 12:3 (KJV)

Our Creator has given every man the same measure of faith. So, for you to move the mountains you are facing in your life, you have to exercise your faith by working your faith muscles. I remember when my young granddaughter was born into this world. She was born perfect and has been such a joy in my life. She entered this world with all the muscles she needs to help her live a healthy life. The muscles were already inside of her little body, and she won't be receiving any more muscles. As she grows older her muscles must adapt to the movements of her body. Her muscles will grow through exercise.

Let's think about this in comparison to our faith. Faith is a muscle, and it will grow when it is exercised. The first use of our faith muscle is when we accept Jesus Christ as our Lord and Savior. "To exercise faith in the Lord Jesus Christ is to accept Him as our Savior and live in accordance with His will through repentance and obedience to His commandments. Learning to act in accordance with one's faith in Christ is fundamental to enjoying deep, life-changing victories."[1] We'll talk more about faith for salvation in chapter three. This is the beginning of our faith walk.

What I want you to understand is that we all have been given the same measure of faith, like Mr. Atlas, we must learn how to grow our "faith muscles" as well as study and understand how each element of our faith works. Just like Mr. Atlas studied the human body to take himself from a weakling to a world class bodybuilder, you too must be willing to find out how your faith works and how to use it to live the life God promised you. Quite honestly, we can't blame our Heavenly Father when we don't use our rightful authority to command our situation to change.

---

[1]   "Exercise Faith," BYU-Idaho, https://www.byui.edu/learning-model/exercise-faith#:~:text=The%20Active%20Power%20of%20Faith&text=3) (accessed 01/27/22)

As you read this book, think about what you have been doing with your measure of faith. Have you been cultivating it and growing it by feeding it the right nutrients or have you been allowing the cares of this world to consume you? The middle part of faith, the part that comes after the enthusiasm wears off, is where you must find your stride and decide in your heart that you won't quit until you experience your healing, financial breakthrough, your relationship restored or whatever it is you are asking God for. Building your faith muscles will prepare you for the journey ahead.

CHAPTER TWO

A Paradigm Shift

URING THE 1920s to 1950s, it was a tradition and a staple of the American family to gather in the evening and sit at the dinner table. These events symbolized the importance of family unity by sitting and eating together, while sharing each other's experiences that transpired throughout the day. The precious moments with family were considered important and valued by families so much that they would often wait to eat until every member of the family was present. This tradition does not remain in many homes today. Over the past 10 or more years, the way we connect with family has changed with the ever-growing world of technology. Although I don't always agree that a fast-paced world is good in every aspect, I do appreciate that I can connect with my family from anywhere in the world at any time. In the early 1900s families connected around the dinner table and those that couldn't make it missed out. But today, this is not the case. With the push of a button on my phone I can connect with my loved ones via video chat. In fact, since the COVID-19 pandemic, many families could not connect in person and had to learn to adapt to the new way of reaching out and seeing each other. Now I am sure everyone hasn't made the switch so effortlessly. I am sure there were people that were so stuck in the way old connections were made, that they missed out on the opportunities to experience their loved ones via technology. The world as we know it is rapidly changing. If we are not adapting with how life has changed, we will be stuck in what used to be. In order for us to accept and adapt, a paradigm shift must take place.

Paradigm: A dramatic change in methodology or practice.[2]

For you to overcome and win in this life there must be a paradigm shift of the normal way of operation. Walking in faith is not something that makes sense in our natural way of thinking. A carnal mind will constantly remind us of what we can't do, it will cause us to focus on how bad our situation is. When we speak about building our faith, it's best that we start at the foundation of our thinking. This is the first step to ensuring we don't lose hope in the middle part of our faith journey.

---

[2] "Paradigm-Shift Meaning," Your Dictionary, https://www.yourdictionary.com/paradigm-shift, (accessed 01/29/22)

A paradigm shift changes the way you think and how you see or view a situation. It is a 360 degree turn around from how you would have responded with old programming versus a new or broadened outlook. A paradigm is a driven agent by which a change must take place to accommodate your future events.

In order to live a successful life, full of victory you must change your natural, physical and spiritual strategies to produce a positive change in your life. You must program yourself to see opposition as an opportunity through God's power and perception through the Word of God. It is my prayer that this book will cause you to shift from the old programming in your life with new programming that is discovered in the Word of God. The old paradigm will keep you stuck in bondage and broken with no forward momentum. That old programming will limit you from fulfilling your purpose. If you do not have a paradigm shift you will remain in a holding pattern, unable to take off or land. You will feel disenchanted with your life and the body of Christ. You will feel as if you are on a downward spiral with absolutely no help.

A paradigm shift will help you bring focus and balance in your life to the extent you will see yourself as God sees you:

- Victorious
- More than a conqueror
- Blessed coming in and blessed going out
- The head and not the tail

- Above only and not beneath
- Going over, and not under

> ❝ The thief cometh not, but for to steal, and to kill, and to destroy: I am come that they might have life and that they might have it more abundantly."
>
> John 10:10 (KJV)

In John 10:10, Jesus first mentions how our life looks before we have a paradigm shift. When Jesus comes into our lives, He becomes the Lord of our lives and our circumstances. A life without Him is one that is constantly losing. It's a life filled with stolen opportunities and dead things. But in this same scripture, He also talks about supernatural life and power that He brings to help you win and dominate in your life. This victorious domination comes as a result of a new paradigm shift.

When you shift your thinking, you do not live in the same old negative and destructive manner, you don't live defeated. John 10:10, part B refers to what I call the zöe life. This is the life that changes the way you see yourself; it is the life that moves you from faith to faith. It is the life that says nothing is impossible for you. This is the life you are looking for. We all have a lot of old programming in the files of our minds, old habits, old practices, old values, old beliefs, and old expectations. This programming determines how you act and react and creates your world around you. To get rid of all these old programs you must concentrate on the Word of God to heal, deliver, and set free.

Meditate on this:

> Jesus Christ can illuminate your vision in such a way that it becomes evident of the difference between the action of Christ and the action of the Devil. With a paradigm shift, you will begin to think differently and act differently.

As Kingdom Ambassadors, we are the sum of God's creation. We can be everything that God wants and needs us to be. Do you know that God created this world because we are His creations? Do you know that we have full use and dominion of this universe? This means the sun shines because of us. The moon lights up the night because of us, and the stars twinkle because of us. God created the heavens and the earth because of us, and He created the lights in the air surrounding the earth because of us. We can breathe and live on the planet, and He did it just for us. Think about how special you are to God. Let me go a bit deeper into this just for a moment.

- God divided the day from the night to let them be for signs and for seasons, for days and years.
- God divided the waters in heaven from the waters in the oceans and seas and made dry land to appear

- God made the grass and the trees yielding fruit whose seed was in itself, after its own kind.
- God created every herb yielding seed after its own kind.
- God created everything on the earth for everything on the earth.
- God created it at our disposal and made us the keeper of His creations.

Everything I mentioned above is yours and at your beck and call. Do you believe this? If you don't, you must shift your thinking today. Until you understand how important you are to our Heavenly Father you will never accept how much you can accomplish through your faith. Scripture tells us:

> 66 And God said, Let us make man in our image, after our likeness: and let them have dominion over the fish of the sea, and over the fowl of the air, and over the cattle, and overall the earth, and over every creeping thing that creepeth upon the earth."
>
> Genesis 1:26 (KJV)

From the beginning of time, God has given us dominion and controlling power or influence over everything. This includes any circumstance you are facing right now. You have the authority to shift what you are experiencing, even those life events that come into our lives abruptly and unannounced. I want to dive deeper into this verse to bring more revelation.

"Let us" in Genesis 1:26 refers to God the Father, God the Son, and God the Holy Ghost.

When God said, "in our image," He isn't talking about the four fingers and a thumb, or the natural body when He speaks of making man in our image. He is talking about making man a spirit. You are a spiritual being. A spirit being is supernatural and cannot be destroyed. It cannot be manipulated and will always be a supernatural source of power. We were always a part of God; therefore, we are spirit.

And the very God of peace sanctify you Wholly; and I pray God your whole Spirit and soul and body be preserved blameless unto the coming of our Lord Jesus Christ. 1 Thessalonians 5:23

The term "after our likeness" refers not only to your incorruptible Spirit, but also to the incorruptibility of God the Father, God the Son, and God the Holy Ghost. Now there were other humanoids that God created before the antediluvian period, but man was the only creature made after the likeness of God. This means we are the only creatures that can pray and bring God to earth on legal ground. Not angels, not demons, or the Devil was made after God's likeness, they were made in God's image, not His likeness; we are a special class of beings.

Here are some additional scripture quotes for your reference.

Genesis 2: 7- 8 (KJV)

[7] And the Lord God formed man of the dust of the ground and breathed into his nostrils the breath of life, and man became a living soul.

[8] And the Lord God planted a garden eastward in Eden, and there he put the man whom he had formed.

According to verse 7, God put mortal flesh on your spirit man. He knew, loved, and fellowshipped with His creation.

1 Thessalonians 5:23 (KJV)

And the very God of peace sanctify you wholly, and I pray God your whole spirit and soul and body be preserved blameless unto the coming of our Lord Jesus Christ.

According to verse 23, God put human flesh on the spirit man. God the Father knew you would inhabit the earth and that you needed a physical body to live down here on this earth. With this revelation, how you see yourself from this day forward should change. It's through this revelation you should know that you are an unstoppable force for God for nothing can prevent you from manifesting God's power.

To summarize what we have learned in this chapter:

To produce a positive result, you must have a paradigm shift. Without a paradigm shift of the mind, you'll struggle to break loose of stronghold patterns. This will cause you to experience repeated cycles of frustration and failure. Because we're created in God's image, this means we have dominion. God wants us to manifest His Glory and power and he gave us His spirit in order to accomplish this.

CHAPTER THREE

Faith for Salvation

WHAT YOU BELIEVE about your authority, plays a big part in your paradigm directing your future. We have passed from spiritual death unto spiritual life because of the life of God in man's spirit. Although we have not yet experienced all there is to know of the effect the spirit of God has on man's born again recreated spirit, this new paradigm shift will give you more insight and depth into the inner workings of the operation of the spirit. This understanding should open a whole new world of opportunities for you both naturally and spiritually. As new creations, we have been put in a position of power and authority— a position delegated to us by God through Jesus Christ. You are a creator and as a creator you have power and dominion over the spirit of the devil. The power is in your hands. Because you are spirit and made in the image and likeness of God you can be and do what the Godhead can do.

Romans 8:17(KJV) tells us, "And if children, then heirs; if heirs of God, and joint-heirs with Christ; if so be that we suffer with him, that we may be also glorified together."

As we start learning more about the new paradigm, let's address some areas you will need to know more about which includes your authority to bind and loose. As a believer in Jesus Christ, we have been given the authority to overcome and win in every area of our life. But in order to walk in this authority we must have the faith to believe this authority belongs to us and that we can exercise the authority. In our modern-day life when an officer of the law or a governmental figure walks into a room, the people in the room adjust to them, accordingly, giving respect and honor to the person wearing the title. There isn't anything special they need to do to command this authority. The authority was given to them when they accepted their role, authority comes with that title. Now let's look at this from a spiritual perspective. This same concept applies to you. When you accept the title as a Christian or believer, you also accept the privilege, respect, and honor that comes along with the role, but you must first know who you are. Our faith starts with our acceptance of Jesus as our Lord and Savior.

Faith for Salvation

> 66 But what saith it? The Word is nigh thee, even in thy mouth, and in thy heart: that is, the Word of faith, which we preach; That if thou shalt confess with thy mouth the Lord Jesus, and shalt believe in thine heart that God hath raised him from the dead, thou shalt be saved. For with the heart, man believeth unto righteousness, and with the mouth, confession is made unto salvation."
>
> Romans 10:8-10 (KJV)

Our faith begins at the point of our salvation. Romans 10:8-10 can be used in every arena of life. Whether you're praying to receive a thousand dollars or perhaps a million dollars, or trying to receive a new coat, a new car, or a new house, you must confess what you are hoping for and speak out what you desire to receive from God. Your faith will cause it to come to pass. If you reject this teaching you are going to be filled with unbelief. What does unbelief do? Unbelief always resists the power of God operating in our lives. Unbelief takes you backwards to the place your faith began, right there at the altar when you received your salvation. Titus 1:15-16 teaches us that unbelief corrupts our minds and conscience and will ultimately render us worthless in our efforts and endeavors. Unbelief is dangerous to our life because it makes us skeptical, cynical, and fatalistic.

Let's dive back into the scripture discussion, in Romans 10:8-10, which explains what each one of us had to do in order to receive salvation. There is no doubt in my mind, this explains what happened when I became born again. I remember my salvation experience as if it was yesterday. I walked down the aisle of my church, stood in front of the altar, and the preacher laid hands on my head and prayed the prayer for salvation. I confessed Jesus Christ as "my Lord" and savior and "I was saved." After the church service, I returned home and I told my mama, my sister, and my brothers about the experience at the altar. I said to them 'I got saved!' Then, I told all my friends, I am saved, and I was. However, there was no physical evidence to prove that I was "saved" except for my own statement. Over time my actions began to line up with my Words. I stopped doing the things that didn't line up with the Word and most importantly, I believed Romans 10:8-10 in my heart. After repeating those Words out of my mouth, I began to act on God's Word that affirmed I was saved.

In due time I started meditating on righteous thoughts and the evil thoughts dissipated. How did this happen? I stopped entertaining those negative evil thoughts, and I began to replace those evil thoughts with the Word of God. In time the bad habits disappeared, and the good habits surfaced. Why? Because I continued to act on the Word of God concerning salvation and I believed those Words in my heart. By faith, I could trust God to make it possible if I obeyed Him and lived an authentic Christian life! I continued to build my faith muscles as I studied the Bible. Now my born-again recreated Spirit began to dominate my mind and body and I took the proper steps that led me closer to God. I studied and immersed myself in the Word daily and my soul was saved. "*Wherefore lay apart all filthiness and superfluity of naughtiness, and receive with meekness the engraved word, which is able to save your souls.*" *James 1:21(KJB) Romans 12:1* taught me to present my body as a living sacrifice, holy, acceptable unto God, which is my reasonable service.

As I looked at Romans 10:8-10, the word **heart** stood out to me in these passages. I noticed that it wasn't speaking about our human organ that pumps blood throughout our body, but it was referring to my Spirit. As a matter of fact, most of the time when we see the word **heart** in the Bible, it refers to the spirit man or the center of man. It is referring to the spirit part of you. Remember, you are a spirit, and you have a soul which lives inside of your body. Anything that you receive from God, you receive through your spirit man. Think about it this way, your spirit man does not have physical hands that can reach out and receive something, so you must receive it another way. The Holy Ghost is in your born-again recreated spirit, and this is how you receive from God. This is what gives you the ability to believe and then receive.

> "But let it be the hidden man of the heart, in that which is not corruptible, even the ornament of a meek and quiet spirit, which is in the sight of God of great price."
>
> 1 Peter 3:4 (KJB)

Let's look at additional scriptures that align with this.

> "My dear brothers and sisters, take note of this: Everyone should be quick to listen, slow to speak and slow to become angry because human anger does not produce the righteousness that God desires. Therefore, get rid of all moral filth and the evil that is so prevalent, and humbly accept the Word planted in you, which can save you."
>
> James 1:19-21 (NIV)

> "Wherefore lay apart all filthiness and superfluity of naughtiness, and receive with meekness the engrafted Word, which is able to save your souls."
>
> James 1:21 (KJB)

Meditate on this:

Your body and soul did not become born again when you gave your life to Christ. Only your spirit man was affected.

> "And the very God of peace sanctify you wholly; and I pray God your whole spirit and soul and body be preserved blameless unto the coming of our Lord Jesus Christ."
>
> 1 Thessalonians 5:23 (KJB)

Meditate on this:

God instructs us to do something about our bodies.

> "I beseech you therefore, brethren, by the mercies of God, that ye present your bodies a living sacrifice, holy, acceptable unto God, which is your reasonable service."
>
> Romans 12:1 (KJB)

Meditate on this:

He tells us to do something about our soul.

Summary

- Receiving salvation is the beginning of our faith journey
- Faith is released by speaking God's Words
- Unbelief corrupts our mind

CHAPTER FOUR

Faith for Regeneration

❝Not by works of righteousness which we have
done, but according to his mercy he saved us, by
the washing of regeneration, and renewing of the
Holy Ghost.❞

Titus 3:5 KJV

REGENERATION FOR THE believer is a radical change.
Just as our physical birth resulted in a new individual
entering the earthly realm, our regeneration or spiritual birth
results in a new person entering the heavenly realm. Before we
accepted Christ as our savior, many of us lived with few moral
standards. We lived in sin doing anything we wanted to do. In
order to live life, the way God intended us, we must disassociate
ourselves from our old way of living, thinking, and being. If you
have ever tried to commit to changing on your own, without

the help of the Holy Spirit, you have probably encountered this truth about our flesh. No matter how much you want to do the right thing, it's impossible to change our behavior within our own strength. If you don't believe this, try going on a diet to lose weight. Your intentions may be in the right place but that won't stop the cravings you will have for foods that aren't healthy for you. Sure, you may start off doing great in the beginning, but before long you will find yourself eating the things you said you wouldn't.

In 1978, right after my conversion, I joined an organization to support me on my new journey as a new believer. The organization had its way of keeping us involved in prayer and service to the Lord. One of their practices was to sit the new converts on the altar or the front row praying for two to four hours per night during their services. One night, I was tired of spending so many hours in prayer and had the brilliant idea to skip church and go to my friend's home. My friend was so cheap we teased him that he squeaked when he walked. However, that night as I played hooky from church, he was just as liberal as he could be with all of the freebies I wanted. I counted it to be a blessing and I sat there for about an hour partaking in the free spread, but nothing gave me a buzz. Nothing happened. The Lord intervened that night and He did not allow me to become influenced by the power of the devil. The free experiment and psychedelic drugs were the enemy's distractions and his way of keeping me entangled in sin and away from God, but his plans did not work. After about an hour I left and went back to church and sat in the front row - where I belonged. I repented for going over to his house and participating in things I knew I had no business doing. Later that night when I returned home, I received the baptism of the Holy Ghost. I believe it was because I was cleansed by the washing of regeneration and repenting from my sins, the Lord had preserved and watched over me so I would not get tricked by the enemy and fall back into my old ways. I believe God was looking out for me so that I would be able to succeed in my faith journey.

When I was born again, I had already lived 21 years for the devil. During that time, I was controlled by flesh, and I did any and everything I was big and bad enough to do. It was a habit in my flesh to obey it and I was powerless to stop obeying it, but when the power of God came into my life that required me to submit and make a conscious decision to follow the precepts of the Word of God and not go back into the old worldly lifestyle. This regeneration required fighting on my part by quoting the Word of God, fasting, and keeping my mind on Christ Jesus as my weapons to defeat the enemy. There were times when I would be defeated, but I continued to stand on God's Word in John 1:9. "If we confess our sins, he is faithful and just to forgive us our sins, and to cleanse us from all unrighteousness." I learned that if I messed up, I needed to repent and get back into right standing with God. Our precious Father loved us so much that He always forgave us. As I continued to grow in my walk with

God, I learned there were other areas in my life I needed to submit to God also.

Titus 3:5-6,8 (KJV)

⁵ Not by works of righteousness which we have done, but according to His mercy he saved us, by the washing of regeneration, and renewing of the Holy Ghost;

⁶ Which He shed on us abundantly through Jesus Christ our Savior;

⁸ This is a faithful saying, and these things I will that thou affirm constantly, that they which have believed in God might be careful to maintain good works. These things are good and profitable for men.

To live a life of faith, we must be washed by the waters of regeneration. The Word "regeneration" means new birth, reproduction, renewal, recreation, regeneration, hence regeneration is the production of a new life consecrated, and sanctification to God, a radical change of mind for the better. The Word is often used to denote the restoration of a thing to its pristine state. Regeneration takes that old man and sanctifies it. It separates it from the things of the world and presents it blameless before the presence of His Glory. The washing of regeneration is a process and your exodus out of your worldly lifestyle. It happens to everyone that makes the transition from sinner to saint. Old things must pass away, and all things must become new. (2 Corinthians 5:17)

However, this process is harder for some than it is for others, but it must take place. As I continued reading and studying the Word, I began hanging out with the saints more and my desire for the things of the world disappeared and the desire for the things of God grew stronger. Titus 3:7 emphasizes that being justified by His grace; we should be made heirs according to the hope of eternal life.

The aim of the new birth is to be justified or to be made right, by His grace we might become *heirs according to the hope of eternal life*. This is important because we can only become heirs according to the hope of eternal life *if* we are cleansed by the washing of the Word of God by the act of regeneration. This process is the transformation from the old thing to a new thing in Christ Jesus, where sin does not dominate us in lust. Therefore, since you have been made free from the bondage of sin, sin has no more domination over you because Jesus Christ has cleansed you by the washing of regeneration.

> Likewise reckon ye also yourselves to be dead indeed unto sin, but alive unto God through Jesus Christ our Lord."
>
> Romans 6:11 (KJV)

To qualify 1 Thessalonians 5:23, in the context of the subject at hand, let me remind you that you are a spirit, you have a soul and they both live inside of your body. The real you *is* your spirit man. That spirit is the only part of you that can contact God; your physical body and your soul don't have the capability to contact God. *"God **is** a Spirit, and they that worship him must worship him in spirit and in truth." John 4:24 (KJB)*

Why We Need This Sanctification

It is important that we understand the regeneration and the sanctification needed for our faith walk. If we don't walk in sanctification, we give the enemy permission to raise havoc against us. No matter how many faith scriptures you quote, if you have sin in your life or iniquity in your heart you will never be able to persevere during the testing and trials you will encounter. Getting through the middle part of your faith journey and accessing the promises require a life of holiness and submission to God.

> 66 Submit yourselves therefore to God. Resist the devil, and he will flee from you."
>
> James 4:7 (KJV)

To be sanctified means to be set apart to be used for something different. Also, sanctification is part of salvation. 2 Thessalonians 2:13 (NIV) says, *"But we ought always to thank God for you, brothers and sisters loved by the Lord, because God chose you as first fruits to be saved through the sanctifying work of the Spirit and through belief in the truth.*" As believers, we are set apart for the use of God for His purpose and to execute His will. We do His bidding for the sole purpose of His plans and pursuits. This is the believer's act of sanctification.

Additionally, sanctification prepares us to be set apart for the use of God, in the service of the Lord, in whatever capacity God sees fit to use us. Whatever God has called you to do in His Kingdom, serve as unto the Lord. We are all needed in some capacity in the service of God. It is our reasonable service to be ready at all times to serve in the house of God. As a pastor, I encourage our members to make themselves available to those that are committed to building the Kingdom. This can include your pastor, team leader, group leader or mentor, or anyone that God has called you to support. When you submit your will to God, you are ultimately saying, *God, you can use me for your glory.* What I love about God is service to Him does not come without reward.

Lastly, there is one last area I want to address as it relates to our regeneration. Allow me to bring clarity to this scripture and how it relates to the paradigm.

> 66 Being born again, not of corruptible seed, but of incorruptible, by the Word of God, which liveth and abideth forever."
>
> 1 Peter 1:23 (KJV)

The natural seed is a corruptible seed, and the spiritual seed is incorruptible. This means your new paradigm will afford you the opportunity to function and operate in both areas, natural and spiritual, causing you to be a force to be reckoned with. How powerful is that? Knowing your authority is critical. It is the Word of Almighty God that is injected into your spirit man to bring about the new birth in your life. You exercise your authority to put off the old man by using the Word of God to renew your mind through the help of the Holy Spirit. With this combination it is a fixed fight - you cannot lose.

CHAPTER FIVE

Exercising Your Faith

66 How God anointed Jesus of Nazareth with the
Holy Ghost and with power: who went about
doing good and healing all that were oppressed of
the devil; for God was with him."

Acts 10:38 (KJV)

I N 1995, I was called to pray for a friend's wife. She was on
dialysis and her body had retained so much fluid she was
almost unrecognizable. I must admit I thought the prayer was
going to be an all-night prayer session, because the others had
prayed and cried out before my arrival. When I saw my dear
friend, Brother Miller, he looked broken. He had his face in
his hands and you could hear and see and feel the hopelessness
and helplessness in the room. The capital prayer everyone was
confessing was, "if it be thy will God, heal Sister Miller."

Even his dear wife was praying "if it be your will, please heal me." She pleaded her case, "I have lived saved, and I have walked upright before you." she cried. With tears in her eyes, she prayed this ungodly, unscriptural, and unbelieving prayer. Understand, I am not pointing this out to make light of that moment. But I must address that a person can only receive as far as their faith level can carry them. As I stood there boldly in faith, confessing Sister Miller's healing, I leaned on the scriptures found in James 5.

James 5:14-15 (KJV)

[14] "Is anyone among you sick? Let him call for the elders of the church; and let them pray over him, anointing him with oil in the name of the Lord: And the prayer of faith shall save the sick, and the Lord shall raise him up; and if he has committed sins, they shall be forgiven him."

Out of all the prayers that went up to the Father that night, none of the prayers were the prayer of faith. Jesus Came to heal but if you are going to experience His healing power you must be bold about your authority. The Word of God is very powerful, and it also requires wisdom from above to understand and use it. The prayer of faith is persistent, and it does not hesitate to put a demand on God and His Word. It says whatever you are believing is yours right now. As I began to speak to my friends, I asked them to say, 'Thank you God. You are the Healer, and when hands are laid on me and I am anointed with oil, I will be healed in Jesus' name.' That which I thought was going to be an all-night prayer service was met by the presence of the Healer Jesus Christ. When we all got on one accord, we laid hands on her and anointed her with oil. We saw her body deflate as if someone had deflated a balloon right in front of our very eyes. God received the glory out of that situation.

If you desire results and a turnaround in your favor, you must be able to apply God's principle of faith. It's very important to pray with faith unwavering and include His Words to back up your supplications. All oppression, sickness and disease, come from the devil. Jesus healed sickness and oppression when He walked the streets of Jordan and Judea, and he is still healing today. Healing belongs to us as our covenant right, anything contrary to this shows a lack of faith.

> 66 By stretching forth thine hand to heal; and that signs and wonders may be done by the name of thy holy child Jesus."
>
> Acts 4:30 (KJV)

This Bible verse tells us about how we can heal through faith. The Bible also says in Hebrews 13:8 (KJV): "Jesus Christ the same yesterday, and today, and forever." That means he doesn't change, and His Words stand forever.

Our Kingdom Authority

What I have witnessed is that many believers do not know their authority. Instead of operating from a faith perspective, as if what they are believing for has already been done, they fear what they are asking for won't happen for them. They waver in their faith, especially at the middle of the faith journey. I can't emphasize enough how important it is to focus on the things we can't see- the promise, instead of focusing on what we can see- the trial. If you don't learn to daily set your sights on what God has promised you, as told through His word, your faith will fail.

Matthew 21:21 reads,

> Jesus answered and said unto them, Verily I say unto you, If ye have faith, and doubt not, ye shall not only do this which is done to the fig tree, but also if ye shall say unto this mountain, Be thou removed, and be thou cast into the sea; it shall be done.

It's encouraging to know that Jesus gave us all authority through his death on the cross, not some authority but all. This means the battle you are in, whether it is spiritual or natural, you have the authority to withstand and come out on the winning side. But there is a catch to this. Jesus's death on the cross does not mean you don't have to do what is necessary to increase your level of faith. Surprisingly, many believers do not understand they have authority in both heaven and earth to stand in the authority of Christ. These same believers think so little of themselves that one would think the Father and the Son weren't in their lives. God's power is in His Word. He is upholding all things by the Word of His power. As believers we need to learn and understand how to walk in authority. To activate this authority, you must come to a full understanding that God dwells in you, and you have an inheritance which includes authority.

Faith for Spiritual Gifts

In 1993, I was holding a meeting in Kansas City, Kansas at a pastor friend's church. The Lord was there and blessed the message, as a result, several people gave their lives to Christ. When the preaching was finished, I was led to minister to anyone that needed healing. I asked if there was anyone that needed hands laid on them to receive their healing. Some people stood up and came forward. Suddenly as I was laying hands on the people, I saw in the Spirit realm as if a movie reel started to play out in front of me about everyone's life that I was laying hands on. I was able to tell them things that were going on in their lives, but only what the Holy Spirit revealed to me. This continued for about 30 minutes with 10 to 15 people coming through the line. My mind began to question how it was happening when I didn't know any of those people outside of the pastor and his wife. I had never seen them before. My mind began to question the validity of what I was seeing. I began to question if what

I was seeing was real. Slowly the movie reel began to become blurry and fade away and I could not see it anymore. Well, this had never happened to me before in this way so I did not know if I was to try to make it come back by having the people in the prayer line continue to come forward or if I should stop because I did not see anything else. I felt led to tell everyone the Spirit had lifted. I could continue to pray for them and if God saw fit to show me anything else I would gladly tell them. I prayed for the rest of the people in the line, but God did not respond to me in that manner anymore that night nor any other time since. In that moment I had submitted myself to be used and set apart by God. I now understand it to be the Word of knowledge. The Word of knowledge is often defined as the ability of one person to know what God is currently doing or intends to do in the life of another person. It can also be defined as knowing the secrets of another person's heart.

Another time, I remembered having a dream that was so real I awoke shaking and trembling. In the dream, I was an associate minister at my church and my pastor asked me without any advance warning to bring the message. In the dream I agreed, but as I took the platform in the dream, I noticed that I had no trousers on and it distracted me terribly, but I thought God would help me. Tragically, He didn't, and I bombed terribly. When I asked God why I had no trousers on in the dream, because this concerned me greatly, the Lord answered and said that I was unprepared for the task at hand, so I had to pray and fast as well as study to be ready at all times, as I was set apart for the use of God. Since that dream, God has dealt with me quite a bit regarding this. In some dreams I am without shirts, trousers, shoes, no haircut, or my face is not washed. The Lord speaks to me often in my dreams to relay a message or give instruction to someone, on this occasion the message was to me that I was unprepared for the task at hand, and I am trying to move forward without His help. This type of dream is called a Word of wisdom.

A Word of wisdom is one of the nine gifts of the Holy Spirit that lives in your born again, recreated Spirit that will give you the special ability to receive instant insight, and the divine revelation of the sovereign mind, will, purpose, and plans of God pertaining to future events. It also gives you the ability to properly apply the knowledge that you may already have in a particular situation. When you have a spiritual gift, it will work without any interference from anyone, person, deity, or thing. According to Romans 11:29, the gifts and calling of God are without repentance. If God has graced you with a spiritual gift it will work, whether you are right or not. The gift and the calling works whether you repent or not.

It's important that you know that faith is not just about what you can produce in your life but also about your input into the body of Christ. We briefly discussed this in chapter four, but I thought it would be good to revisit this. It will take faith to walk in your spiritual gifts as well. "Faith is the root of spiritual gifts that depend on and draws the life-giving grace of God. Our spiritual gifts enable us to grow in the knowledge of Christ. Faith is the defining trait of gifts that transforms them from natural to spiritual.

There are Nine Spiritual Gifts Referenced

"Faith draws grace from the river of God's bounty and, by means of spiritual gifts, transmits that grace to others."[3]

> 66 For to one is given by the Spirit the word of wisdom; to another the word of knowledge by the same Spirit; 9 To another faith by the same Spirit; to another the gifts of healing by the same Spirit; 10 To another the working of miracles; to another prophecy; to another discerning of spirits; to another divers kinds of tongues; to another the interpretation of tongues."
>
> 1 Corinthians 12:8-10 (KJV)

As you increase in your faith your spiritual gifts will also begin to increase. If you don't yet know how God wants to use your gifts, seek the Holy Spirit for direction and guidance. Too many believers are sitting on their spiritual gifts instead of activating

---

[3] John Piper, "Faith: the Root and Trait of All Spiritual Gifts," Desiring God, September 12, 2004

them by faith. I believe this has had a negative effect on the body of Christ, causing us to be weakened in signs and wonders. Believers must understand the uniqueness of who God has called them to be. It's because many lack the understanding of their authority, that they fail to reach their full potential in Christ.

CHAPTER SIX

Faith to Create

66 In the beginning, God created the heavens and the earth."

Genesis 1:1 (KJV)

66 So God created man in his own image, in the image of God created he him; male and female created he them."

Genesis 1:27 (KJV)

I N THE BOOK of beginnings, God displayed His power and ability as The Creator. In Genesis 1:26-28, the Bible says God created you and gave you this great power and ability to create and call things into manifestation. The power is in you, and it has been in you from the beginning of time. Maybe you are aware that you have this power, but you don't know how to make it work. You may be frustrated and confused about life's ups and downs. Maybe you have been on a financial rollercoaster, one month you are riding high, and you can't put your finger on why the next month you are down low. Maybe you are unaware of what is going on and don't understand that the ability to create is in you, and you continue to live your life in lack and poverty. There is good news, God has given you the power to change that situation, Isn't that great news?

When we were kids, many of us were bold, courageous, and weren't afraid to do anything. As we grew up, we were taught to limit our expectations and not shoot too high so that we will not be disappointed. Does this limit God? He isn't a God of mediocrity; He is the God of more than enough. He wants us to ask "anything" and with faith, it's made possible. His desire is for us to live a life that expresses His Glory, but do you think being mediocre expresses God's Glory? Certainly not!

God is the largest energy field that makes up the entire universe as a whole. The Bible says we are made in His image and His likeness. This means you are an energy field also. Not as big as God, but an energy field, nonetheless. What is the energy field? It's something that moves in and out of form that cannot be created and cannot be destroyed. The Heavenly Father has no beginning and no end He moves in and out of form to master His universe.

God Called You a Creator

Meditate on these scriptures

(As it is written, I have made thee a father of many nations,) before him whom he believed, *even* God, who quickeneth the dead, and calleth those things which be not as though they were. Romans 4:17

66 While we look not at the things which are seen, but at the things which are not seen: for the things which are seen are temporal; but the things which are not seen are eternal."

2 Corinthians 4:18

Mark 11:22-24 is an instruction directly from Jesus to us. He tells us to speak to the mountains that we face in our lives. He didn't say, "Beg God to move the mountain." He said you speak to the mountain. The problem that many of us have today is that we are speaking about the mountain, but we're not speaking to the mountain. We are spending our time complaining about how bad things are instead of changing or shifting the atmosphere. In any unwanted situation, after you have prayed, you must exercise your authority over that situation in Jesus' name, As a child of God?

Did you know everything you have now you have called it into your life? What you are experiencing now is a result of yesterday's thoughts and actions. You are a powerful force and God has invested so much into you including the power to create. You are a work of art, you are a masterpiece, you are divinely and spiritually designed, you are created and crafted in His image, and if He is a creator then you are a creator also.

This power or "gifting," as I like to call it, is always at work. It is working as you are thinking all the time. It never stops, you can't put it on pause, you can't rewind it, and you can't fast forward it. It is working while you are sleeping. It is always on. This is why everyone needs to know how it works. It works through you because Christ is in you. You have that special something on the inside of you that was deposited at the beginning of time, this creative ability is in you that you can do greater work for the kingdom. But it takes a few more steps to activate this greatness that is on the inside of you, then you must learn how to control it in your life.

Then you can manifest the prosperity, love, happiness and anything else you so desire into your life. There is nothing you need to purchase, it is already in you, but the key is recognizing who you are. You may ask yourself *who am I?* Let me answer that for you...

- You are a powerful magnet.
- You are a powerful energy field.
- You draw every thought you think and speak to you.

Remember the key is controlling your thoughts and ultimately your words. What you say and think goes out into the spirit realm and returns with what you think about or speak about. It doesn't matter whether they are positive or negative thoughts, they will show up in your life. Let me reiterate this, your Spirit isn't biased. If you think negative thoughts and say negative words, those negative results will come back to you. The same is true for positive thoughts. Your powerful, supernatural spirit man will move people, situations and things to bring those things (created by your words) to pass.

> ❝As it is written, I have made thee a father of many nations before him whom he believed, even God, who quickeneth the dead and calleth those things which are not as though they were."
>
> Romans 4:17 (KJV)

Say this out loud, I am a creator!

Now I know this doesn't always feel good to say, especially when your surroundings seem to say otherwise, but force yourself and say it every day because it is true, and the scriptures above give you the right to say it. The things you are reading in this book about you, your spirit man, and God are true and are spiritual laws. The more energy you give to a thing the bigger it gets, the less energy that you give to that same thing you will find it will dissipate. Your great creative power is always on, and always working. You are a powerful force for God so much so that whatever you focus on your Spirit will draw that thing to you and it will show up in your life.

66For as he thinketh in his heart, so is he."

Proverbs 23:7 (KJV)

The levels to which you think will make anything you think about possible. Meditate on that! If you can control your thought life, you can manifest into your life anything in the world and beyond. Controlling your thoughts means you do not linger on negative and destructive thoughts, and you definitely do not give negative thoughts life by speaking them out of your mouth. Now that you are aware of this power and ability to create your world around you, you will think good and happy thoughts knowing that the things you are thinking about will come about according to Mark 11:23-24.

Meditate on this:

You hold everything in your spirit man and you must learn how to control your body and your soul by your spirit man.

The Bible tells us in 2 Corinthians 2:5, to cast down imaginations, and every high thing that exalteth itself against the knowledge of God and bring into captivity every thought to the obedience of Christ. You must focus on your thoughts and concentrate on the positive and get rid of all negativities and don't allow anything to the contrary to enter your mind.

> 66 Finally, brothers and sisters, whatever is true, whatever is noble, whatever is right, whatever is pure, whatever is lovely, whatever is admirable--if anything is excellent or praiseworthy--think about such things."
>
> Philippians 4:8 (NIV)

****

> 66 Be not deceived; God is not mocked: for whatsoever a man soweth, that shall he also reap."
>
> Galatians 6:7

Your spirit man will make your dominant thoughts come to pass in your life because of the investment that God has placed on it. Keep in mind your spirit man does not know if you are just joking around or if you are serious about the words that you are thinking or speaking; it does not ponder the difference between the two. Let me also add this, the more passion you have for something the faster it will show up in your life. If you send out hate and curses on a person, it will boomerang back to you and you will get back hatred and curses. On the other hand, if you send out love, respect, and honor you will reap love, respect, and honor. This is a spiritual law and it is an exact law, which means it will not fail nor change. It will work all the time and every time. Your spirit man is like a garden. Whatever you plant will come up. Naturally, if you plant watermelon seeds in your garden you are going to grow watermelons every time without fail; additionally if you plant hemlock in that same garden right next to your watermelons you will get deadly poison every time without fail. The soil does not know or differentiate what type of seed was planted, it just does what soil does to make the seed you plant manifest. Just like the garden of your Spirit, whatever you plant in your spirit man will also grow every time without fail. Be careful! Don't ever forget that your thoughts control your life. As God's creation, you have the ability to create things.

CHAPTER SEVEN

Faith and Your Ability to Believe

ETWEEN WHERE FAITH begins and ends, there is the middle part of faith. My greatest intent in writing this book is to have you so stirred up that by the end, your faith will grow so much you will act on what you believe in every situation. Throughout this book I have provided you with scripture references to help you build your faith. As you continue to read, meditate on these scriptures for more insight and revelation from the Holy Spirit.

In this chapter we will take a deeper dive into scriptures and give you a more in-depth study into what we have been discussing. Knowledge of the Word of God along with its proper application will build your faith. In those moments when you don't know how to move or you get discouraged remember what the Word says about your situation.

John 14:1-15

¹ Let not your heart be troubled: ye believe in God, believe also in me.

² In my Father's house are many mansions: if it were not so, I would have told you. I am going to prepare a place for you.

³ And if I go and prepare a place for you, I will come again, and receive you unto myself; that where I am, there ye may be also.

⁴ And whither I go ye know, and the way ye know.

⁵ Thomas saith unto him, Lord, we know not whither thou goest; and how can we know the way?

⁶ Jesus saith unto him, I am the way, the truth, and the life: no man cometh unto the Father, but by me.

⁷ If ye had known me, ye should have known my Father also: and from henceforth ye know him, and have seen him.

⁸ Philip saith unto him, Lord, show us the Father, and it sufficeth us.

⁹ Jesus saith unto him, Have I been so long with you, and yet hast thou not known me, Philip? He that hath seen me hath seen the Father; and how sayest thou then, Show us the Father?

¹⁰ Believest thou not that I am in the Father, and the Father in me? the Words that I speak unto you I speak not of myself: but the Father that dwelleth in me, he doeth the works.

¹¹ Believe me that I am in the Father, and the Father in me: or else believe me for the very works' sake.

¹² Verily, verily, I say unto you, He that believeth on me, the works that I do shall he do also; and greater works than these shall he do; because I go unto my Father.

¹³ And whatsoever ye shall ask in my name, that will I do, that the Father may be glorified in the Son.

¹⁴ If ye shall ask anything in my name, I will do it.

¹⁵ If ye love me, keep my commandments.

Jesus said in John 14:12, to believe in Him and the works that He does you will also do; and not only that, greater works than the ones you have read about in the Bible because He went back to the Father. This gives me the impression that Jesus is giving me the authority to believe.

Authority means: A person or organization having power or control in particular situations the power or right to give orders, make decisions, and enforce obedience.

Belief means: To act as if it has already been done, to accept something as true or feeling sure of the truth of a thing.

In John 14, Jesus had told His disciples of His impending departure. He told them He would be with them a little while longer and where He was going, they could not go. I am sure this came as a shock to them as they had been following Jesus and heavily relied on His leadership, teachings, and ability to perform miracles, signs and wonders. This is why they needed to know that they were able to continue to believe in Jesus even after He ascended to the Father. Jesus was the centerpiece of their lives, and they knew there was still so much work to be done. They had begun to do the works of Christ, which consisted of preaching, teaching, and healing. They had to believe in Jesus in every aspect of His lives. The disciples had very serious work to do, and I believe Jesus was aware of the need for them not to lose faith in Him or the works that He had done as is written in part B of John 14:11, *"Or else believe me for the very works' sake."*

Jesus is reminding them to continue believing in Him and that He and the Father are one. And if they can't believe that Jesus and the Father are one, then at the very least believe Him for the very works that he had done in which they had witnessed. Remember they were afraid, and Jesus their leader had just told them He was only going to be with them a little longer. You will notice the constant reassurance to believe and remember Jesus Christ:

> ❝ Let not your heart be troubled: ye believe in God, believe also in me".
>
> John 14:1(KJV)

Jesus knew they were troubled about His leaving, the reassurance by Jesus further illustrates the importance of their need for Christ after He was gone. We as believers also must remember our relationship with the Master and the works that He did.

Jesus Christ has given all things unto us if we believe in Him and in His works. In the middle part of your faith journey, it is going to be imperative that you follow the leading of the Lord and just like the disciples were encouraged to believe in Jesus, the Word of God is speaking to us as we read and remember Christ. The things that He has done, we should apply them to our everyday life on this faith journey.

The disciples were "in front of the cross" and "behind the cross." What I mean by in front of the cross is before the crucifixion of Christ. Because He had not died and He had not risen from the grave and no blood had been shed, therefore there was no remission for sins: "And almost all things are by the law purged with blood; and without shedding of blood is no remission [for sin]." Hebrews 9:22 (KJV)

Behind the cross is where the early church was born. This was after Jesus had risen from the dead and appeared to Mary and his disciples. Let's discuss this more in depth to help you better understand. I will use the Apostle Peter as a reference for this. We are familiar with the story of Peter denying Jesus three times. This occurred in front of the cross, or before the crucifixion. Peter denied Jesus before Jesus died and therefore, according to Hebrews 9:22 without the shedding of blood, there is no remission for sin.

In John 13:38. Jesus answered him, wilt thou lay down thy life for my sake? Verily, verily, I say unto thee, the cock shall not crow, till thou hast denied me thrice. Peter did exactly that.

- First - Peter denied Him at the door of the temple. John 18:17

- Second - Peter denied Him at the fire where he stood and warmed himself John. 18:25
- Third - Peter denied Him to the servants of the high priest and immediately the cock crowed. John 18:26, 27

I believe Jesus offered restoration and forgiveness to Peter for his denying Him. This was now the third time Jesus appeared to the disciples after He was raised from the dead in John 21:15.

So when they had finished eating, Jesus said to Simon Peter, Simon, son of Jonas, lovest thou me more than these? He saith unto him, Yea, Lord; thou knowest that I love thee. He saith unto him, feed my lambs.

1. The First Restoration and forgiveness Jesus asks Simon Peter, son of Jonas, lovest thou me more than these? Peter saith unto him, Yea, Lord; thou knowest that I love thee. Jesus said to Peter feed His lambs. John 21:15

2. The second Restoration and forgiveness Jesus asks Peter lovest thou me? he saith unto Him, Yea, Lord; thou knowest that I love thee. He saith unto him, Feed my sheep. John 21:16

3. The third Restoration and forgiveness Jesus said to Peter Simon, son of Jonas, lovest thou me? Peter was grieved because He said unto him the third time, Lovest thou

me? And he said unto Him, Lord, thou knowest all things; thou knowest that I love thee. Jesus saith unto him, Feed my sheep. John 21:17

Jesus authorizes the disciples to believe in Him and not forget the work. The works of Jesus are preaching, teaching, and healing, but none of these things can be accomplished without the knowledge of Jesus Christ. Your ability to believe in Jesus is the most important thing in your faith's journey because without Jesus there is no gospel, there is no salvation and no healing power. Jesus is the centerpiece of this generation, He is the hope for this world's ills.

Everything starts with Jesus but it is our responsibility to carry out the work. The Bible tells us that all things are possible to those who believe. Knowing about faith and living a life full of faith all comes down to what you believe. Do you believe that Christ died so that you could have an abundant life? Do you believe God has mansions in store for you? Do you believe that every trial is working together for your good? Do you believe in God and in Him you live, move, and have your being? What do you believe? Now before you answer those questions, I can look at your life and tell you what you believe. Your life is a direct result of your beliefs and no matter what you say, the world you have framed around you will tell what you really think. After we accept faith for our salvation, and we walk on our regenerated sanctified journeys, it doesn't stop there you must believe.

I want to encourage you to build your faith to believe the impossible so that the miraculous will be evident in your life. I have so many stories that I can share with you about how my faith turned impossible situations into testimonies. The money that God has placed in my hand, and the businesses he has provided to me make me be a good steward over it because I constantly activate my faith to believe.

Mark 11:22-24 (KJV)

22 And Jesus answering saith unto them, Have faith in God.

23 For verily I say unto you, That whosoever shall say unto this mountain, Be thou removed, and be thou cast into the sea; and shall not doubt in his heart, but shall believe that those things which he saith shall come to pass; he shall have whatsoever he saith.

24 Therefore I say unto you, What things soever ye desire, when ye pray, believe that ye receive them, and ye shall have them.

Belief means to accept (something) as truth. It is to feel sure of the truth, of what you believe, then act in accordance with it. If your reaction to God asking you to believe a thing is, "I don't have any proof or I can't see it with my eyes, or what if it doesn't come to pass," you must remember that God has given you the ability to believe. He has done everything He is going to do and He has given you all the power and authority you need on this earth to act on His Word. Therefore, since His Word is truth and whatsoever you shall ask in faith, He is obligated to give it to you, as long as it lines up with the Word of God. Your Words as a believer carries weight in the spiritual realm as well as in the natural realm.

> 66 Verily I say unto you, Whatsoever ye shall bind on earth shall be bound in heaven: and whatsoever ye shall loose on earth shall be loosed in heaven."
> Matthew 18:18 (KJB)

As a believer, you have the capability of commanding both earth and heaven with God's approval. I know this may seem obnoxious to you, but I am telling you the truth. If you believe the Word of God and stand on it by faith without doubting it will become reality to you. I am not saying there will not be opposition trying to discourage you from reaching your destination by bringing doubt and unbelief, I would be remiss if I didn't tell you this, *yes*, there will be opposition. Yes, there will be an affliction to challenge your beliefs but if you hold fast to your confession of faith without wavering in the name of Jesus it will work. Let me repeat this. Jesus has done all He is going to do and although He is seated at the right hand of the Father, He has given you power over the devil in the name of Jesus.

> 66 Behold, I give unto you power to tread on serpents and scorpions, and over all the power of the enemy: and nothing shall by any means hurt you."
>
> Luke 10:19 (KJV)

The ball is in your court. Jesus Has passed it to you and all you must do is act on what you believe and stand your ground and act like it is so in the name of Jesus. Whatever the problem or the circumstances, it does not matter, stand your ground. You are more than a conqueror in Him, you simply must say that you are, and the things you are trying to manifest will come to pass.

> 66 These things I have spoken unto you, that in me ye might have peace. In the world ye shall have tribulation: but be of good cheer; I have overcome the world."
>
> John 16:33 (KJV)

Do you follow where I am going with this? God has given us His Word, and it has multiplying principles. You need to read it and find out what belongs to you. And when you read it and find out what belongs to you, you don't have to ask Him for credentials. You just need to believe it like you believe anything else. When you got saved. You believe in your heart the Lord Jesus and confess with your mouth that God has raised Him from the dead, like you did when you stood on the Word to land that job, or your friends, or your new church, or your new relationship. It is the same principle you believe in your heart you confess with your mouth and the things you are praying for shall come to pass. This new boss of yours could be right and fair, but behind closed doors, he may be the most ungodly person around. But you have chosen to have confidence in him, despite the fact that you don't know him. Why would you have confidence in him? I will tell you why! You have confidence in him because you can see him with your eyes, you can hear him with your ears. But God, you cannot see with your eyes, and you cannot hear with your ears and these factors make it difficult to believe in God for some people.

You have the capacity to believe God, even when you cannot see Him. Many times, we may become flesh ruled because we are motivated by what we see, as well as what we are trying to do. It is my intention to aid you in becoming more spiritually minded. To receive from our Heavenly Father, you must be spiritually minded.

CHAPTER EIGHT

Words Can Kill Your Faith

Have you ever heard anyone say, "Well I didn't really mean what I said?" I was joking around. Or they may say, "It's not a big deal, I didn't really mean that." It is a popular response, whenever people ask, "Do you have any money?" and your reply is "Nope, I don't have any money." Some people reply this way because they either do not have any money, or they really don't want to give that particular person any of their money. But did you know that when you say you don't have any money, but in fact you do, what you are really doing unknowingly is making a confession of faith? This would be classified as an idle word.

Matthew 12: 36-37 (KJV) says, "But I say unto you, that every idle word that men shall speak, they shall give account thereof in the Day of Judgment. For by thy words thou shalt be justified, and by thy Words thou shalt be condemned."

If you are speaking haphazardly without consideration of what you are saying, you are out of line with God's Word and as a consequence, "every idle word" you speak is going to be given an account of. Once again, let me reiterate! Every idle word that comes out of your mouth is going to be counted. God is a God of principle. When we want to receive from Him, we must follow the same principles.

Notice what the Bible says in Matthew 12:37 (NKJV), "For by your words you will be justified, and by your words you will be condemned." To be justified means to be made right. Let's go a bit further, by your own words, you're going to be made right and by your own words, you're also going to be condemned. As a result, you'll have whatever you say, whether negative or positive. I can't emphasize this enough, whether it's negative or positive you are going to have the results of what comes out of your mouth. Is this easy to control? No. However I am firmly convinced, you can keep your mouth and thoughts under control by casting down every thought, and every imagination, that exalts itself against the knowledge of God; including everything that stands in your way that seems greater than the Word of God that you speak.

The negative thoughts and negative words you speak will become your reality so these actions must be cast down. As soon as those thoughts rise up, they need to be cast down. If the Bible says you can have what you say when you pray, speak, mutter, and you expect it to come to pass then you must believe that you have already received it, this is believing in the immediate response.

Consequently, the text in Matthew 12: 36-37 (KJB) says you are going to be condemned or justified by the words that come out of your mouth, these passages of scripture should give us more reason to speak words of faith, at all times and in all situations watch what we say.

Let's check out the meaning of condemned, so you may understand the urgency of being careful to speak words of faith, at all times and in all situations.

Remember even in folly, playing around, and joking can cause you to become bound up by your own words. Another example is saying, "Now I'm so scared I'm going to die." Other negative idle words I often hear people say are "Man, you're wearing me out," or "You make me sick."

Why would you want to become "worn out" or "sick?" Often these words slip out of our mouths unattended and nonchalantly because they have become embedded within the soulish realm of our DNA, our mind, will, and emotions. Remember, all of these are words that have come out of your mouth, and if you choose to continue to repeat these types of words, they will manifest in your life; you will eventually get sick, you're going to eventually die, because you are speaking death to your life, repeatedly over years. Do you want to die prematurely? I don't think that you do. Understand that your words are powerful; your words carry weight because the Holy Spirit is your power source.

"And the Word was made flesh, and dwelt among us, (and we beheld his glory, the glory as of the only begotten of the Father,) full of grace and truth." John 1:14 (KJV)

Meditate on this:

Your Words will become flesh and they will show up in your life because you are calling them to do so, good, bad or ugly.

Now I need to address something here and I don't mean to offend you, but it must be said. Many times, when people are going through difficult situations, they ask for others to pray for them. Because I am a pastor, I receive many of these types of calls. I don't mind praying for **the people of God but I must say that** as badly as I want you to be healed and delivered, you will have to believe the Word and watch what you say for yourself. Sure, I would like for every person that I lay hands on or pray for to be set free and whole. I have also realized that although we may want something badly for someone else, because the faith walk is an individual experience, this means my faith will align with your faith but it can't supersede your faith or your actions. Whatever you say out of your mouth is going to come to pass or happen for you, my prayers can't cancel this. Consequently, you cannot desire a particular thing for someone else, unless they are in agreement with what you are hoping for, on their behalf. It does not matter how badly you want them to be healed, delivered, or any other type of blessed state.

Let's take for example, someone you know is dealing with a sickness in their body. They say they are waiting on God, but they haven't done anything for themselves. They have not even tried to get out of the bed on their own and they have people coming over to their house to visit, bringing food and medicine and waiting on them hand and foot. Although they say they want to be healed, their actions say something different. Sadly, many people like this have started to enjoy getting spoiled from all of the attention and oftentimes they stay stuck there. Can you see the picture I'm painting here so far? You cannot force them to receive their healing. You cannot force anything on them. That is why the scripture says "whosoever", because it only applies to the individual who reads the Word, believes the Word and stands on their own faith and applies it. Faith in the Word of God always works for those that apply the Word to their lives individually. Go ahead and make this declaration, "I'm going to be careful about what I say because I know that whatever I say is going to be faith-filled words."

If I believe I can have whatever this Bible says is for me, then I must be careful not to say anything that is going to jeopardize my promises. I also must keep my mouth closed, especially under pressurized situations. Refusing to say idle words about my destiny, about my life, and about the things that I am desiring to receive from God requires discipline and practice. I know in doing so, whatever I say is going to come to pass.

You should put into practice speaking the Word of faith to every situation in your life. You must also read, believe and apply the Word of God. You are what you eat, and the more you eat on the Word of God, the more you will bear its fruit.

CHAPTER NINE

Say What the Word Says

> 66 But what saith it? The word is nigh thee, even in thy mouth, and in thy heart: that is, the word of faith, which we preach."
>
> Romans 10:8 (KJV)

FTEN WHEN A crisis arises, people complain and fuss while having so many negative things to say about the situation. It will almost bring you to tears if you hear them, venting their frustrations, dislikes, and their disgust. I have heard believers ask the question "Can't I vent?" My reply to that is, "Yes, if you want more of the same results." As a spiritual magnet (the spirit part of you), whatever you plant with your words will come to pass in your life. Your spirit is like a garden. You can plant tomatoes, and you can plant hemlock in it, and both will come up. One you can eat and the other is a deadly poison, but both will come up in the same garden. The moral of the story is your spirit does not care what you plant; whatever you plant is going to come up in your life.

Let us look again at Mark 11:22-24 (KJV)

²² And Jesus answering saith unto them, Have faith in God.

²³ For verily I say unto you, that whosoever shall say unto this mountain, Be thou removed, and be thou cast into the sea; and shall not doubt in his heart, but shall believe that those things which he saith shall come to pass; he shall have whatsoever he saith.

²⁴ Therefore I say unto you, what things soever ye desire, when ye pray, believe that ye receive them, and ye shall have them.

These scriptures confirm that the soil of your spirit man, whatsoever you plant good, bad or ugly will come up or come to pass; your spirit is not discriminatory.

Let's look at Galatians 6:7 again:

⁷ Be not deceived; God is not mocked: for whatsoever a man soweth, ***that shall he also reap.***

Every "shall" in the Bible is loaded with purpose, possibility and power and will come to pass. Shall is a positive fact, which means that "it" will happen.

One of the problems many people have is they are constantly talking about what is going on at the moment in their current situation. They say what they see with their natural eyes, but this is the opposite of faith. Throughout the previous chapters, I have been teaching you about faith principles in order to help shift your terminology, change your words, and make you mindful of how you speak. I want you to be careful to change how you act in the middle of adverse circumstances. In the middle of your storm, it could be the sight of the mountain standing in your way. Let me be clear, there will be mountains in your way most of the time. Whatever you decide to accomplish will come with a mountain experience. Somebody or something is going to try and stop you. Why is that? Because the Bible says that we have an adversary, and he is the devil. So, if the devil is our adversary, then he is automatically against us and he wants to discourage us. He can't stop you. He can only discourage you and make you sad, but he doesn't have any authority or power over us, hence you have a choice to either get liberated or remain stuck and discouraged.

A few years ago, I was in a conversation with an acquaintance; he said, "can't nobody stop the St. Louis Rams but the Rams." He was talking about the American football team as they were having one of their best seasons. They were faced with a lot of opposition but their team kept rising to the occasion. We could say nobody can stop the believer but the believer. The devil can't stop you. If you are saying what the Word of God is saying over your situation then you're on your way to triumph.

Hebrews 4:12 (KJV)

"For the word of God is quick, and powerful, and sharper than any two edged sword, piercing even to the dividing asunder of soul and spirit, and of the joints and marrow, and is a discerner of the thoughts and intents of the heart."

For the next few pages, I want to place emphasis on the power of the spoken Word of God. We know that the world was framed by His Words. It's the power in His Words that have the ability to create. Because His spirit lives on the inside of you, you possess this same power. But do you really know how powerful The Word is?

The Word of God is the only thing that can separate the spirit and soul, I repeat, the only thing that can separate the spirit and soul is the Word of God. I repeated this because I want you to think about this for a minute. In some cultures, there are different ingredients used to make ink, but dye and oil for the most part are the two main ingredients that will make ink. It's not like you can't use other colors and other components to make it but once you mix the dye and the oil together there is no way to undo the situation. This is how powerful the word of God is; it has the capability to divide asunder the soul from the spirit, not only that it can divide asunder joints from the marrow. I used the oil and the ink to illustrate the impossibility of these situations, but the Word of God can make the seeming impossibility possible. If you look at it from this perspective, the Word of God will deliver you from any situation and any circumstance if we can only say what the word says in the middle of your faith journey.

The Word of God is Alive

The Word of God is alive. Hundreds of people can be in a church service and the Word of God can speak to each individual as the preacher is preaching and they individually may understand something different about that particular message as it relates to them. The Lord is able to speak through his Word to every person in attendance because of the power of the Word and the ability that's in the Word of God.

The Word of All-Knowing Knowing

God is omniscient, meaning He's all-knowing. God is omnipresent meaning He's everywhere present at the same time God is able to get His message to where it needs to go, regardless of who you are and where you are. Your reading this book right now is evidence of His commitment to reaching you and how far His Word will go. The Word of God to you is the message of Faith, hope, deliverance and salvation. Whether you are getting the Word by watching a television program or sitting in a church service, God is able to communicate with you because of His presence. It is because of this truth that we can rest assured that He knows how to reach us.

The Word was There in the Beginning

John 1:1 (KJV)

"In the beginning was the Word, and the Word was with God, and the Word was God. The same was in the beginning with God. All things were made by him; and without him there was not anything that was made. In him was life; and the life was the light of men. And the light shineth in darkness; and the darkness comprehended it not."

Genesis 1:1

"In the beginning God created the heavens and the earth and the earth was without form and void and darkness covered the face of the deep." Before darkness covered the face of the deep, the Word of God existed, so the Word was around prior to the earth being covered with darkness. Therefore, as long as we put confidence in the

Word and say what the Word says over your situation, you cannot go wrong. The Word has been here forever. The Word created everything. The Word is Jesus. Jesus was with God from the beginning and He is still with God.

God's Word and redemption is the greatest gift God gave to humanity. That is why it is important to read the Bible and hear the Word because it can speak to you about your circumstances at any time or moment. I know there are a lot of books to be read, and even this book that you are reading can help but it should not supersede the Word of God. The Word of God is the one that gives us life, and if you noticed I'm supporting everything that I'm talking about with the Word. The Word of God has the perfect answer to your circumstances. All you need to do is ask yourself, "What is God saying concerning this situation?" For example, if you're sick, He has told us that by His stripes we are healed! Isaiah 53:5 That's all you need. You need to always speak God's Word over your life, and circumstances, and this will also help you pray with so much clarity and direction.

Isaiah 55:11 (NASB)

"So will My Word be which goes out of My mouth; It will not return to Me empty, without accomplishing what I desire, And without succeeding in the purpose for which I sent it."

Matthew 24:35 (KJB)

"Heaven and earth shall pass away, but my Words shall not pass away."

God honors His Word more than His name. When you speak His Word, you're reminding God of His promises or holding Him accountable. The Word of God is so perfect! It has the answers to all of your questions. Jesus is wrapped up in the Word and he never sleeps nor slumbers and He's always concerned about you. He's always thinking about you and looking out for you therefore whatever situation or circumstance you find yourself in, you need the Word of God. Wherever you are in life, you must submit yourself to God. By focusing on His word, He will perfect all that needs perfecting in your life and change your circumstances. You can win through the Word.

As you are in the middle part of faith, the Word is what you need to sustain yourself. No matter what type of report you hear. It can be a negative report from the doctor. Or maybe a spouse that is leaving after twenty years of marriage. It can be a child that does not want to be obedient. It does not matter what the situation may be, the Word is just what you need to keep you in the fight. Standing on the Word and promises of God is a sure deal. His Word cannot lie and it cannot fail. What a guarantee we have when our words come into alignment with God's Word. This is what faith will do. It will cause you to speak the impossible and see it become possible. Your hope is not in your words alone, but in the power of the Word of God.

> 66 And we know that all things work together for good to those who love God, to those who are the called according to His purpose."
>
> Romans 8: 28

God has already given you the answer key, to whatever it is you want. Mark the 11:21 says,

"Verily I say unto you that whosoever..." Guess who He is referring to in this scripture. You! Yes, you are whosoever! It doesn't matter who you are, what side of the track you come from, what color you are, what continent you reside on, or what your family origin is. None of these things matter. "Whosoever shall say unto…" What's that thing that's stopping you?

"Whosoever shall say unto this mountain be removed!" You've got to be bold enough to know that you have the power, the ability and the wherewithal to speak to that thing and tell it to move!

God is clear. He has given you clear instructions if you are a believer. Because you are a believer, He is your perfect substitute. He substituted His life for your life and now, whenever you say something out of your mouth it's like God's saying it. Whenever you begin to speak, the demonic forces hear you talking. They know this is the Son of God talking. Why is that? They hear the Lord when you speak. If you are a believer, God lives in you. That's why the Bible says, "Greater is He that is in you than He that is in the world." 1 John 4:4 (KJB) My aim is to explain to you that you can speak to the monstrosity of that mountain, the thing or situation that's in your way and it has to move. Think of the bully at the playground. He is going to intimidate you and mess with you because you won't fight. But he doesn't know that you've got an elder brother and as soon as he figures out you do, after you go home and get him, he's going to stop messing with you. But unless you remind him about your big brother... everyday... everyday he will keep taking your lunch money. The only way to stop the bully from taking your lunch money is to recognize your ability and the power source that's on the inside of you.

Is His ability lying dormant on the inside of you? Are you using the power you have been given and using your words to shift atmospheres? The power lies in your hands, what are you going to do with it? I want to encourage you to use the power. I believe that when we do not use the power of the Word of God it's an insult to God because he has invested so many great things in us. He gave us His only son, who He loved greatly. He has even given us the power of the Holy Ghost, He has recreated your born-again spirit. He has changed your life, so don't insult Him by living life as if you do not know Him or have His ability on the inside of you. I want to encourage you through this book to start today to realize and understand that you have the power, you have the ability, and you have the resources to change your life and the lives of those that you have influence over.

The way to do it is to start acting like you have the power to believe, start acting like you have the ability to change your circumstances. When I say act like it, I mean believing as if it is done. You have to imagine yourself with the thing that you're believing God for. You have to imagine yourself driving that car. You have to imagine yourself with the power to lay hands on the sick and they shall recover. When I say that you have to see yourself laying your hands on the sick, imagine you are there doing the praying not somebody looking like you. I'm talking about seeing yourself through your own eyes actually doing the thing you are believing God for because you have the ability to make it happen. God has given you this ability.

I was speaking to a friend not too long ago and I was explaining to her that Jesus has done everything that He is going to do for mankind. He has suffered, bled, and died a criminal death, while on a criminal cross. He took your sins and took them to God who has equipped us with virtually everything we needed to do His will and to live a life that pleases God.

Believe The Word

Believers tend to say, "I'm believing God for this or that." Oftentimes, what we're really doing is substituting the word believing for wishing or wanting. When you say you're believing God for something, what is it based on? It should be based firmly on His Word. [4] Just because you need or want something, doesn't mean you're believing. The next time you hear yourself say, "I'm believing," pause a moment and examine yourself.

> 66 But without faith it is impossible to please him: for he that cometh to God must believe that he is, and that he is a rewarder of them that diligently seek him."
>
> Hebrews 11:6

Believing in the resurrected Christ leads to salvation but, to please God, what we believe has to be put into practice by a "pattern of imitation and inheritance." John Piper says that imitation begins with our relationship with God. As Piper puts it, "God is pleased by us when two things about him are reflected in our relation to him. One: that he is real; and the other: that he is rewarding. We see that "the vitality of faith is rooted in what God is like, not

---

[4]   "Is Your Faith Real? 5 Ways to Examine Your Faith," Kenneth Copeland Ministries, April 3, 2021, https://blog.kcm.org/faith-real-5-ways-examine-faith/, (accessed 12/22/21)

what we are like." Yet, "the more you know what God is like, the more conformed to his greatness will be your faith."

[5]Understanding that God rewards the faithful that draw close to Him, but faithfulness leads us to actively and outwardly imitating the One we trust. By an act of faith, Enoch skipped death completely. "They looked all over and couldn't find him because God had taken him." We know on the basis of reliable testimony that before he was taken "he pleased God." It's impossible to please God apart from faith. And why? Because anyone who wants to approach God must believe both that he exists and that he cares enough to respond to those who seek him.

Meditate on this:

Make every effort to supplement your faith with virtue, and virtue with knowledge. 2 Peter 1:5

Faith Comes by Hearing the Word

There is a big difference between having heard and hearing. Revelation comes from allowing and expecting the Word of God to be quickened to your spirit and change you on the inside.

---

5   Candace Lucey, "What Does 'Without Faith it is Impossible to Please God' Really Mean?" Crosswalk, (5/15/20),
     https://www.crosswalk.com/faith/bible-study/what-does-without-faith-it-is-impossible-to-please-god-really-mean.html, (accessed 1/13/22)

That's why it is important to fill up on the Word of God every day by reading it and listening to teachings.

> **66 Don't assume that because you're saying you're believing, you really are believing."**
>
> Pastor Keith Moore.

Keep renewing your mind and building your faith until you feel your faith boiling over. Then, and only then, is it time to say, "I'm believing." When you're dealing with a problem with your health, finances, a relationship, or your job, you must first ask yourself, *"What does God's Word say about my situation?"* Because that's the last word. Giving the Bible first priority means that you go to the Bible first in each issue or circumstance. It means you're searching to see what God says about it before you consult with friends, family, or the internet. It means that in any scenario, His Word is the final word. The Bible provides spiritual fuel for your spirit. It strengthens your faith and makes you ready for anything.

"So then faith comes by hearing, and hearing by the Word of God." Romans 10:17 (NKJV) The Bible is as essential to your life as food is to your survival, you are depositing into your spirit life when you feed on the Word on a regular basis, and this creates a reserve. You can't wait until there's a problem before working on your faith. You must constantly work on your faith by meditating on God's Word so it'll be on your spirit. Where the will of God is known, faith begins. If you don't know what His Word says, you can't have faith in it. After you've learned God's will and spent time meditating on it, you can put it into practice by exercising authority over your life.

After you've immersed yourself in faith, applying God's Word to your situation will become natural. Total immersion is the finest approach to learning faith. When you immerse yourself in a faith-filled environment and make faith your only language, it will serve as your first line of defense in every situation.

Faith and Love

> 66 That Christ may dwell in your hearts through faith; that you, being rooted and grounded in love."
>
> Ephesians. 3:17(NKJV)

> 66 And the grace of our Lord was more than abundant, with the faith and love which are found in Christ Jesus."
>
> **1 Timothy 1:14 (NASB)**

Faith and love have a complex relationship. You can't walk in pure God-designed love without first walking in faith, and you can't walk in faith without first walking in love. Study God's Word to learn more about this connection, and how to live it. When you combine love with faith, your entire perspective changes, and you begin to see the world through our Heavenly Father's lenses. When faith and love exist together, it is proof that we have genuinely been reborn. Both faith and love can be linked to Christ's unity. We are linked to Christ by faith. We become curiously and gloriously connected to Him when we believe in Him. Christ's life seeps into ours. And it is His life in us that gives us loving hearts, for our brothers and sisters in Christ. Christ, on the other hand, adores His followers. Those who are in Him and share His life will therefore, undoubtedly be loving, as he was. When we love God, trusting and believing in Him wouldn't be a hard thing to do.

We have discussed quite a lot in this chapter, so allow me to give you some more takeaways to help you in your journey.

Remember that venting is not a spiritual practice.

Faith is exercised through speaking what you believe into existence.

Faith is exercised by speaking the Word of God in any situation at all times.

Do not waver in this, keep speaking what you know to be truth, your spiritual truth is God has equipped us with everything we need in His Word, it is your responsibility to become immersed in it because without faith, you can't please God.

You must fill up your heart with the Word of God daily. There's a Word for every circumstance you encounter.

CHAPTER TEN

The Middle Part of Faith

B EFORE WE CLOSE this book, I want to tell you how much of an honor it has been to share my personal experiences of faith with you. As I was writing this book, I thought about the countless people that I have prayed for and counseled over the past twenty years of ministry. There are so many believers that are getting stuck in the middle part of their faith journey, and they are giving up. I remember colleagues in the faith, similar to my friend, who have left this world before they experience God's manifestation. These are good people that believe in God, who Satan has robbed of their inheritance.

Many of those conversations I've had with people of God have ended with them saying words like, "I don't think I am going to make it" Or "This is just too hard of a test for me." I had to write this book because I didn't want that to be your story. It's not uncommon for believers to stop just before they are about to receive their breakthrough and it saddens me. Many of God's people are not experiencing the good life, the life of abundance and full of joy that Jesus mentioned throughout the New Testament.

Why do Believers Have a Hard Time in the Middle of Faith?

There are too many believers that have a hard time in the middle. Let's think about this as if it were an ocean. If you are a good swimmer, going deep into the ocean is a comfortable place for you. However, if you are a beginner, venturing into the deep can be intimidating. As you venture deeper into the water, the seashore becomes harder to see and the color of the water turns into a deeper shade of blue. What's the purpose of this example you might ask? The seashore represents your comfort zone, and the water represents the new things or depth in the old things God has called you to do. It is the unfamiliarity that believers struggle with, in the middle part of faith. I know it may look like you would sink, but God would not allow you to sink. You have to believe that God wants the best for you.

Applying the Principles

The principles of faith apply whether you are praying for yourself or someone else. In both instances, you must believe you will receive when you pray and stand on the words you say. The topic of healing is still a controversial one today. Some people just simply do not believe healing is for us today in the conventional sense. They do not believe it is God's perfect will for people to be healed. However, the Bible is clear on the matter. I still believe in healing. I also believe that we can receive healing not just in our physical bodies but also in our minds and our emotions as well.

How to Pray With Faith

The first and most important thing about faith is you must believe that you'll receive a result when you pray. You can't pray about something and then immediately worry about what the outcome will be. Trust that your Heavenly Father will never leave you.

There are seven (7) key points to know to be able to pray with faith. F.E Marsh highlighted some important steps to take when praying with faith, which include:

1. Confession of sin. "To seek by prayer and supplications." (Daniel 9:3-20)
2. Cleansing from sin. "Thy sin purged." (Isaiah 6:7)
3. Consecration to the Savior. "Behold, he prayeth." (Acts 9:11-20)
4. Confidence in the Savior. "Said unto the Lord, increase our faith." (Luke 17:5)

5. Courage from the Savior. "They lifted up their voice to God with one accord." (Acts 4:24-33)
6. Calmness in the Savior. "The peace of God...shall keep your hearts and minds." (Phil. 4:6-7)
7. Communion with the Savior. "Did not our heart burn... while He talked with us." (Luke 24:32)[6]

These steps bring us closer to God and also help us manifest the power of the Lord. If you have been missing the mark, don't stay where you are. If you need to repent, do that and dust yourself off. This is another opportunity for you to get it right. As a teacher sometimes my tone can be a bit tough because I want the best for you. I want you to draw near to God and allow Him to keep you and sustain you. You don't have to fight this battle with your own strength. The Word tells us that His strength is made perfect in our weakness. God has mapped it all out for us. Sometimes as humans we tend to take the hard road, but if we stick to what God has commanded us to do, and don't veer off the path, we will experience the reward.

Staying Committed to the Vision

In the middle part of faith, always remember if your current state or circumstances do not reflect the image God has shown you in your visions, dreams or prophetic word over your life, the

---

6   "Prayer of Faith," Blue Letter Bible, https://www.blueletterbible.org/Comm/ marsh_fe/bible_readings/312.cfm, (accessed 3/11/22)

promise still awaits you. When Joshua went to spy out the land, he saw the great things God had in store and was able to bring evidence and give a good report. The Almighty will allow us to taste a portion of the promise, but He will take us back to be processed. In the middle part of faith stay committed until what God has promised manifests in your life.

Remaining Hopeful of the Fulfillment of the Promise

As believers when we become discouraged, we have to remind ourselves of the promises of God. Sometimes it helps in these cases to have childlike faith. What do I mean by that? If you have ever had an experience with promising a child something you know just what I'm referring to. They never let you forget what you have promised. As long as they don't see the promise they give you gentle or not so gentle reminders of what you have said. They are relentless and do not give up until they receive their prize. That type of faith is what you and I need to have in the middle of our faith journey. A relentless, persistence to go fully through the process to receive the promise.

Doing What is Needed to Shift Your Environment

If you are looking to make it through the middle, you cannot surround yourself with persons who are murmuring and complaining about their middle. You also can't be around people that speak fear over faith. That type of atmosphere actually begins to affect and dampen what you are believing in God for. You would have allowed people to come and rain on your parade. You need people who are going to be a ray of sunshine. This type of atmosphere is present when we worship. There may be times when you enter a church feeling heavy, but because of the corporate anointing and grace in that house, during worship, you become engaged and connected to your Heavenly Father, and the spirit of heaviness lifts off of you. You begin to feel a surge of strength and energy to keep going. Another good practice to shift your environment is to allow the scriptures to play out loud in your atmosphere. The sound waves of the Word of God traveling through your atmosphere will shift your environment. In the middle part of your faith journey, strength for the journey is required. Be strong and of good courage.

Staying the Course

If you are going to stay the course and make it through the middle, there are three (3) key points you will have to incorporate in your life.

Prayer

Prayer is communicating with God. In the middle part of your faith journey, consistent and persistent prayer is required. Be like Jacob in Genesis 32:26 "I will not let you go until you bless me."

Jacob refused to let the angel go until he had received the promise. Prayer gives you peace in the middle of your faith journey, it gives hope in the middle of your faith journey. In prayer, God can give you new strategies and revelations to make it through the middle part of the faith journey.

Connect With a Body of Believers

The Bible reminds us in Matthew 18:20 (KJV) "For where two or three are gathered together in my name, there am I in the midst of them." When you are in the middle of faith and your faith tank is low, God gives us a blueprint to build our faith back up for the journey. Being amongst a body of believers can strengthen you in the middle. Their presence, grace and wisdom can be encouragement to go through.

Find a Scripture That Fits Your Situation and Hold Fast to It

The Lord honors His Word. Meditate on God's Word pertaining to your situation. The Bible reminds us to stand on His Word. God is actually saying to you My word is the strongest foundation you will ever encounter. You will not find a crack or leak in His Word. You can rest assured that if you lean on the Word, the Word will hold you up.

Unlocking Faith for Your Next Level

God's desire for us is to keep growing not only in faith but in every sphere of our lives. He loves it when we keep advancing in glory and power, and one of the ways to activate this is through faith. In order to move to the next level, you must be able to know the level you are currently at, what your desired next level is and how to unlock your faith for the next level. Being a believer does not rule out the fact that you need to admit and critically look inward to review your growth. You need to face the reality of your current situation and be ready to deal with it. You may struggle with moving to the next level if you don't admit the level you currently are at. Some believers think that because God has given us the access to faith, we don't need to put in effort to stimulate the faith.

We can't sit on our faith and do nothing, like an unused skill. We must demonstrate our faith by acting. It can be frightening to take a risk and try something. We can trust God to work things out for our good because we have faith in him. Take for example, you need a job but you don't send a resume, attend interviews or offer to intern with your company of your choice, how do you expect to get a job? God is not a magician and he expects us to do our part.

You don't need to be embarrassed while admitting your current situation, this step is very crucial to unlocking your next level.

Everything you want in life and out of life is already in seed form in you and God will bring it forth only as you "walk by faith" and trust Him for the impossible.

Self-Reflection Exercise

Is there an area in your life you need to work on? Write these areas out with all honesty.

Knowing Your Next Level

Your next level is dependent on where you are and where you are ultimately destined to be. There needs to be a total reawakening to realize your full potential and to understand where you're destined to be. With faith you can discover your next level and ultimately live a life that resembles God's glory. Since you've admitted where you are and what your situation is, the next step is how to unlock faith for the next level.

Unlocking Faith

The Bible tells us faith is a gift from God. Ephesians 2:8 Through his compassionate grace, God gives us the very thing we need to follow him. Faith is the path to God. We need only follow it.

Listen to the Gospel in Romans 10:17 and believe in Jesus as your Lord and Savior. You've read in His Word about all the wonderful things faith can bring you (deliverance, health, wealth etc.), but you're baffled as to how to put that faith to work for you. You have two options at this point: either ignore your faith and hope for the best or devote some time to learning how to apply it. Faith becomes unlocked and effective when it is built on a strong foundation of accurate answers (truth), when you believe in the integrity of that truth, when you trust in that truth, and when you are hearing that truth on a continual basis. The "truth" in this context is the Word of God.

To unlock our faith for the next level, we need:

- A word from the Lord that answers our problem.
- Our words in alignment with the Word.
- Our actions must correspond with the Word or promise we are hoping for.

James explained this principle well.

James 2:20-24 (NIV)

[20] You foolish person, do you want evidence that faith without deeds is useless?

[21] Was not our father Abraham considered righteous for what he did when he offered his son Isaac on the altar?

²² You see that his faith and his actions were working together, and his faith was made complete by what he did.

²³ And the scripture was fulfilled that says, "Abraham believed God, and it was credited to him as righteousness," and he was called God's friend."

²⁴ You see that a person is considered righteous by what they do and not by faith alone.

The assurance of the promise or the truth, together with the passion, determination, and conviction with which we adhere to these faith principles, will not only sustain but also fire up our faith, putting pressure on the spiritual realm to manifest what we are believing for in the natural realm. You need to put in some effort to stimulate your faith, and to move to the next level, you need to know the level you are currently at. Faith becomes effective when built on the strong foundation of God's Word. Faith is released by speaking God's Words. Because we are believers, our Words and our requests must line up with the Word of God.

Here are the four (4) steps to help you move forward and activate your faith:

1) Ask according to the Word.
2) Believe the Word
3) Speak the Word
4) Stand firm on the Word.

Now faith is the substance of things hoped for, and the evidence (or the proving of things not seen with the natural eye). Hebrews 11:1

I pray that this book has been helpful for you. I also pray that it strengthens you so that you can endure the race God has set before you. As I have expressed throughout this book, you are not alone. The Holy Spirit was left as our comforter to lead us and teach us all truths. This isn't the time for you to give up or tap out. This isn't the time for you to speak negative words or allow others to speak against what you know God has said. I wrote this book to help you build your faith muscles to face the giants that stand up in your life. Through God by faith, there is nothing you can't do. There is no mountain you can't cast into the sea. There is no problem too big for your God to solve. Do you believe it? I pray so. The ball is in your court. Now go and win in the name of Jesus.

WORDS FROM THE AUTHOR

Hello, my name is Reginald McNeese

I am the president and founder of Word of Life Spoken Word Ministries, where we teach people how to be healed by the Word of God. God has given me a mandate to teach the faith to the body of Christ with a strong emphasis on healing. Our focus is to introduce the Word of God into the lives of the hearer to bring life to that part of the body through the avenue of faith.

My healing school classes have left a lasting impact on the students that attend these sessions. I have, with the help of the Holy Ghost, revealed another look at Christ as it was given to me by the Holy Ghost. This revelation knowledge is on the cutting edge of Spiritual integrity. I am not saying it's anything new, but it's definitely revealed knowledge from the throne room in heaven and I am honored that God has given me this revelation knowledge for this time.

I am a 1993 graduate of Rhema Bible Training Center, graduating in the Pastor's class with an emphasis in Evangelism. I have Ministered extensively in evangelistic crusades across the country with emphasis on healing. Our annual Spirit of Faith Conferences brought knowledge to the body of Christ as the Word of God, through faith, was taught by powerful men and women of God.

I also foundered and was the Senior Pastor of Harvest Church of Illinois in Belleville, Illinois, where we taught and built the members in exercising their faith in God; He worked miracles in the body and our members grew in their faith.

Harvest Church of Illinois in its humble beginnings was birthed in 2005 out of my apartment and it grew from there. Our youth and children's ministries drew kids from the community that enjoyed games and challenges that directed them to Jesus. We were able to bless the community with meals on Sundays and help our community with toys for tots. We also partnered with the local prison system where the inmates could spend time in our church services on occasion to elevate a portion of their time in the system.

We partnered with the United Way to bring low-cost transportation for the elderly that did not meet the States mandate or qualification. This low cost and in some cases, free transportation extended to doctors' appointments, pharmacy runs, and blood drops. It also included limited grocery stores and dry cleaners visits. We also partnered with our local Catholic charities to provide hotel stays with meals for families with small children in the winter months. As a community Church, Harvest Church of Illinois we were the go to ministry for families with small children that were in need.

We were able to secure a lucrative contract with the State of Illinois and Missouri in an effort to become a greater help to our community in the greater St Louis area, by being on a list of providers for Nonprofits, ministries, and Churches to help its residents with delinquent utility bills, ranging from water, gas, and electric, and some time court fees and fines.

Harvest Church of Illinois and Harvest Transportation Service Inc. played a tremendous role in these endeavors by employing ten to fifteen people and securing eight to ten vehicles. This put Harvest Church of Illinois in the middle of the action in our community and in the surrounding metropolitan area. We are grateful to the Lord for having been instrumental in His endeavors to enhance the lives of His people in our communities.

As we move forward we have a new name but the same mandate, *TEACH MY PEOPLE FAITH* but with an emphasis on Healing.

Mark 11:23-24 (KJV)

For verily I say unto you, that whosoever shall say unto this mountain, be thou removed, and be thou cast into the sea, and shall not doubt in his heart, but shall believe that those things which he saith shall come to pass; he shall have whatsoever he saith.

The Word of Life Spoken Word Ministries illustrates the power of the Spoken Word that makes the impossible possible. This book is just one of the instruments that expresses the vision that God has given. Please look forward to more books in the very near future.

The Word of Life Spoken Word ministries is a ministry that travels from city to city, from church to church, holding what we call healing school classes. Our focus is **teaching you how to be healed by the Word of God** by actually applying the Word of God to your symptoms to create a healing and a cure.

This is the same technique Jesus used when He walked the earth.

Matthew 4:23 (NKJV)

And Jesus went about all Galilee, teaching in their synagogues, preaching the gospel of the Kingdom, and healing all kinds of sickness and all kinds of diseases among the people.

Thank you for purchasing my book.

Reginald McNeese
Connect with me: www.reginaldmcneeseministries.com